bride tribe

a memory book

SIP SIP HOORAY

a bachelorette party
memory book

I DO
crew

the details

The Bride To Be: _____

Maid of Honor: _____

Bridesmaids: _____

_____

_____

Location: _____

Date of Party: _____

Date of Wedding: _____

BEFORE

the party...

AFTER
the party...

life

was meant for

good
friends

and

great
adventures

memories

kiss the miss

Leave a kiss for the miss and sign your name.

goodbye

so we don't
forget...

Favorite songs: _____

_____

_____

Favorite drinks: _____

_____

_____

Favorite quotes: _____

_____

_____

memories

memories

memories

a

l i t t l e

party

n e v e r   h u r t

nobody

memories

memories

memories

memories

memories

these are the DAYS to REMEMBER

memories

memories

memories

Manufactured by Amazon.ca
Bolton, ON